HAWAI'I SINGS

A creation of aloha
for the children of Hawai‘i.

Mahalo nui loa
Nathan Napoka, Hana Pau,
Kendrick, Geoffrey,
Maile and Aunty Alma
for believing in possibilities
and dreams.

To Kellie and Blaine,
for their endless supply of
encouragement, support
and love.

Copyright © 1995 by MnM Books, an imprint of
Mutual Publishing
Illustrations © 1995 by Doug Po‘oloa Tolentino

Design: Hans Loffel

First Printing December, 1995
1 2 3 4 5 6 7 8 9
ISBN 1-56647-083-8

Mutual Publishing
1127 11th Avenue, Mezzanine B
Honolulu, Hawaii 96816
Telephone (808) 732-1709
Fax (808) 734-4094

Printed in Korea

Hawai'i sings

Written by Joy S. Au
Illustrated by
Doug Po'oloa Tolentino

At the beginning of time, it was dark.

Then the sun warmed the earth.

And from the sea, life came to the land.

People were born,
And in time
They found the islands.

From far away they came.
To sing and dance
And to play
To the beat and rhythm
Of the sea and land.

Dance with me, called the sea.
Dance with me,   called the land.
Dance with me,   called the wind.

And tell of this special place
Called Hawaiʻi.

From the roaring reef, came *pū*.
Mahalo ... kai.

From the whispering shore, came *'ili'ili.*
Mahalo ... 'āina.

From the rustling coconut grove, came *pahu* and *pūniu*.

Mahalo ... niu.

From the crawling vines, came *ipu.*
Mahalo … ipu.

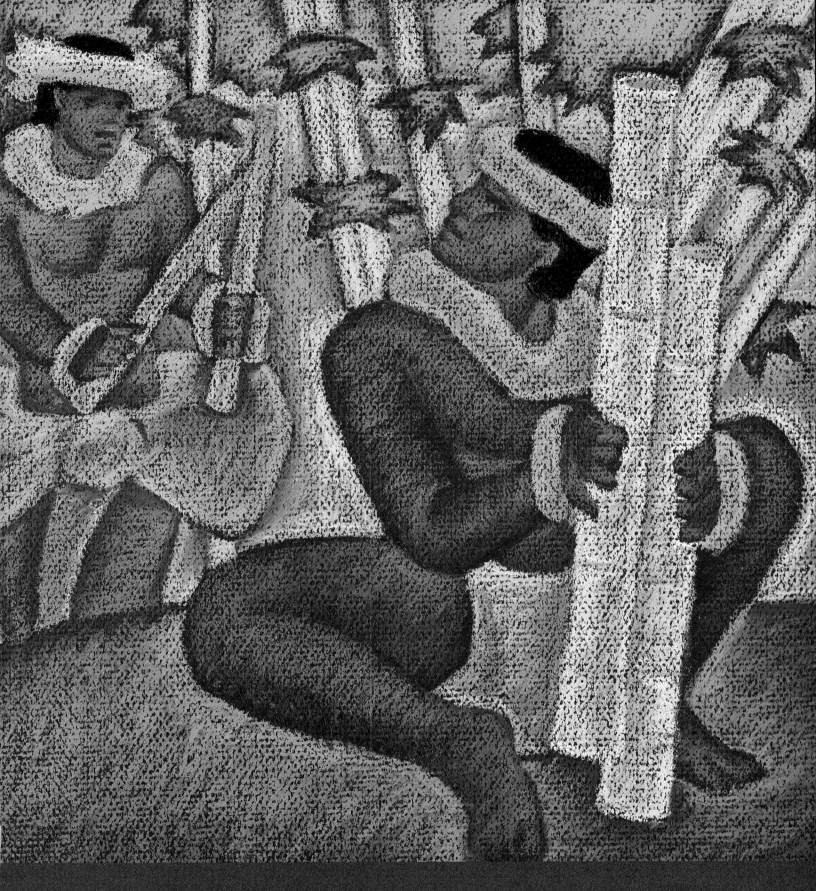

From the swishing bamboo patch, came *pūʻili* and *kāʻekeʻeke*. *Mahalo ... ʻohe.*

From the quiet forest, came *kā lāʻau*
Mahalo … lāʻau.

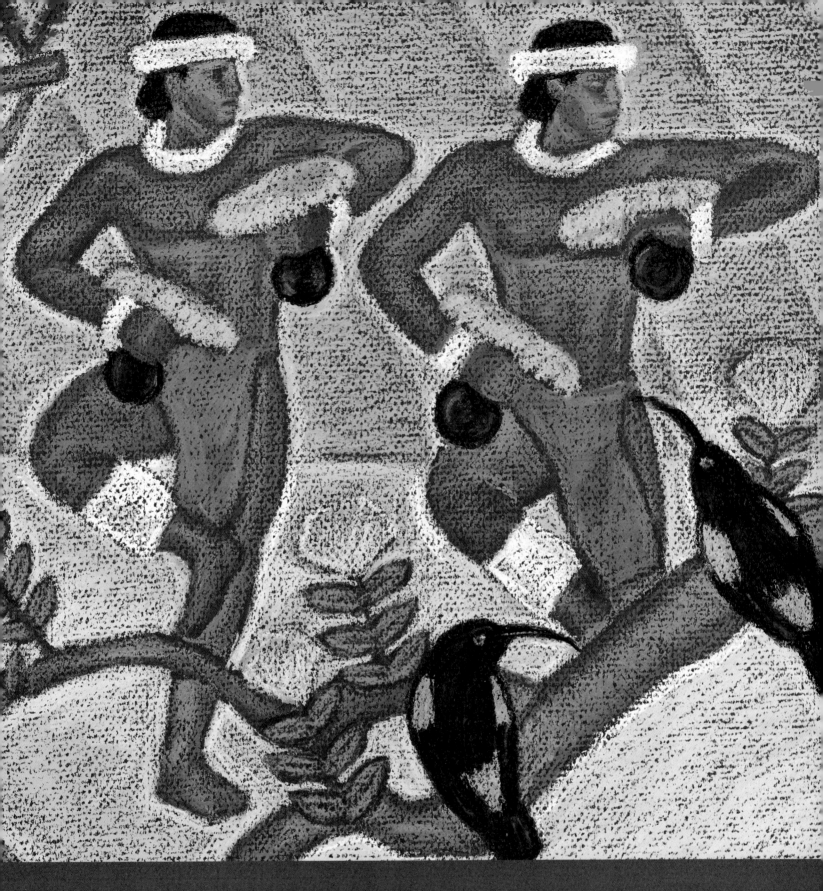

From the singing birds, came *ʻulīʻulī*.
Mahalo … manu.

From the high mountains came the wind.
It filled the people with *aloha*.
It filled their hearts with song.

Mahalo i ke Akua.

Dance with me,   called the sea.
Dance with me,   called the land.
Dance with me,   called the wind.

And sing a *mele* of Hawai‘i.

GLOSSARY

'Ili'ili

Ipu

'Ohe

Pahu

'Āina is the land.

Akua means God, the Divine.

Aloha refers to love and is a greeting of friendship.

'Ili'ili are small smooth water worn stones used
   as percussion instruments.

Ipu refers to the bottle gourd vines. The gourd is
   cleaned out and used as a percussion instrument.

Kā'eke'eke is a bamboo piece with an open end used
   as a percussion instrument.

Kai is the ocean.

Kā lā'au are wooden rhythm sticks.

Lā'au refers to plants, trees, forests and wood.

Mahalo means thank-you and refers to gratitude.

Manu refers to birds.

Mele means a chant or to sing.

Niu means coconut.

'Ohe refers to the bamboo plant.

Pahu is a drum made from a hollow tree trunk.

Pū is a large conch shell used as a wind instrument.

Pū'ili is a bamboo rattle.

Pūniu is a small knee drum made from a coconut shell.

'Ulī'ulī is a gourd rattle topped with feathers.

Pū

Pūniu

'Ulī'ulī

Kā lā'au

Pū'ili